Anonymus

Report of the Proceedings of the Numismatic and Antiquarian Society of Philadelphia

For the Year 1883 with Necrological Notices

Anonymus

Report of the Proceedings of the Numismatic and Antiquarian Society of Philadelphia

For the Year 1883 with Necrological Notices

ISBN/EAN: 9783741198007

Manufactured in Europe, USA, Canada, Australia, Japa

Cover: Foto ©Suzi / pixelio.de

Manufactured and distributed by brebook publishing software (www.brebook.com)

Anonymus

Report of the Proceedings of the Numismatic and Antiquarian Society of Philadelphia

REPORT

OF

THE PROCEEDINGS

OF

THE NUMISMATIC AND ANTIQUARIAN SOCIETY

OF PHILADELPHIA

FOR THE YEAR 1883

WITH NECROLOGICAL NOTICES

PHILADELPHIA
PRINTED FOR THE SOCIETY
1884

THE NUMISMATIC AND ANTIQUARIAN SOCIETY OF PHILADELPHIA.

FOUNDED JANUARY 1, 1858.

1884.

OFFICERS.

President.

ELI K. PRICE.

Vice-Presidents.

DANIEL G. BRINTON, M. D., EDWIN W. LEHMAN,
WILLIAM P. CHANDLER, LEWIS A. SCOTT.

Honorary Vice-Presidents.

MASSACHUSETTS,	HON. ROBERT C. WINTHROP,	Of Boston.
RHODE ISLAND,	HON. JOHN RUSSELL BARTLETT,	" Providence.
CONNECTICUT,	ASHBEL WOODWARD, M. D.,	" Franklin.
NEW YORK,	J. CARSON BREVOORT, Esq.,	" Brooklyn.
NEW JERSEY,	HON. WILLIAM A. WHITEHEAD,	" Newark.
DELAWARE,	HON. THOMAS F. BAYARD,	" Wilmington.
MARYLAND,	HON. JOHN H. B. LATROBE,	" Baltimore.
DISTRICT OF COLUMBIA,	PROF. SPENCER F. BAIRD,	" Washington.
VIRGINIA,	R. ALONZO BROCK, Esq.,	" Richmond.
GEORGIA,	CHARLES C. JONES, Jr., Esq.,	" Augusta.
LOUISIANA,	JOSEPH JONES, M. D.,	" New Orleans.
ILLINOIS,	HON. ISAAC N. ARNOLD,	" Chicago.
WISCONSIN,	PROF. JAMES D. BUTLER,	" Madison.
MINNESOTA,	HON. ALEXANDER RAMSEY,	" St. Paul.
IOWA,	RT. REV. WILLIAM STEVENS PERRY,	" Davenport.
CALIFORNIA,	HUBERT HOWE BANCROFT, Esq.,	" San Francisco.

Corresponding Secretary,	HENRY PHILLIPS, Jr.
Recording Secretary,	R. STEWART CULIN.
Treasurer,	HENRY PHILLIPS, Jr.
Historiographer,	CHARLES HENRY HART.
Curator of Numismatics,	ROBERT COULTON DAVIS.
Curator of Antiquities,	EDWIN ATLEE BARBER.
Librarian,	THOMAS HOCKLEY.

COMMITTEES.

COMMITTEE ON NUMISMATICS.

JOHN R. BAKER,
A. E. OUTERBRIDGE, Jr.,
WILLIAM S. BAKER,
ROBERT COULTON DAVIS, *ex-officio.*

COMMITTEE ON ANTIQUITIES.

FRANCIS JORDAN, Jr.,
WESTCOTT BAILEY,
REV. JOSEPH F. GARRISON, M.D.
EDWIN A. BARBER, *ex-officio.*

COMMITTEE ON GENEALOGY.

PHILIP H. LAW,
JOSEPH H. COATES,
J. HAYS CARSON,
CHARLES HENRY HART, *ex-officio.*

COMMITTEE ON FINANCE.

J. SERGEANT PRICE,
HENRY HUNGERICH,
ROBERT NOXON TOPPAN,
HENRY PHILLIPS, Jr., *ex-officio.*

COMMITTEE ON LIBRARY.

HENRY C. LEA,
G. ALBERT LEWIS,
JOSEPH W. BATES,
THOMAS HOCKLEY, *ex-officio.*

COMMITTEE ON HALL.

ISAAC MYER,
WILLIAM TRAUTWINE,
HARRY ROGERS,
R. STEWART CULIN, *ex-officio.*

COMMITTEE ON PUBLICATION.

HENRY PHILLIPS, Jr., DANIEL G. BRINTON, M. D., CHARLES HENRY HART.

Hall of the Society, Southwest Corner Eighteenth and Chestnut Streets.

Stated Meetings, First Thursday Evenings in January, February, March, April, May, October, November and December.
Annual Meeting, First Thursday Evening in January.

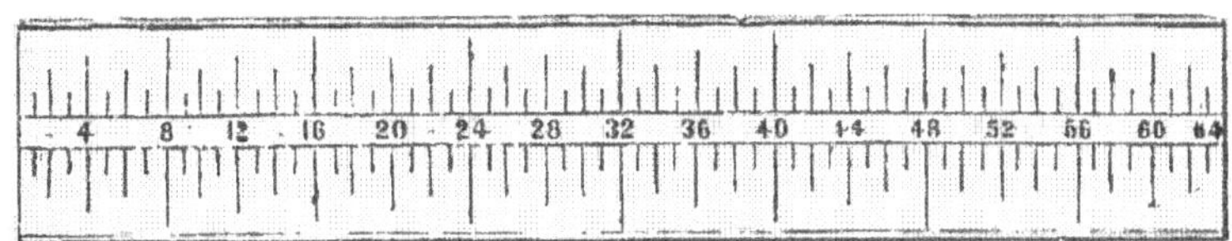

To the President and Members of the Numismatic and Antiquarian Society of Philadelphia.

GENTLEMEN: I have the honor to submit the following report of the operations of the Society for the year 1883. During the year there were held eight meetings, at which eighteen papers and communications were read; six resident and fourteen corresponding members were elected, making twenty in all; three members resigned, and three died. There were donated, books and pamphlets, 278; coins and antiquities, 674; letters received, 213; letters, publications, packages, etc. sent, 1327.

The following is a brief abstract of the more important proceedings of the Society during the year.

JANUARY 4TH.

The twenty-fifth anniversary of the foundation of the Society, (Thursday, January 1, 1858), was celebrated this evening. The proceedings, together with the addresses delivered on the occasion, have been already printed and distributed by the Society.

FEBRUARY 1ST.

Among the donations were the following from Mr. Barber:

Four "Fairy Pipes" from the vicinity of London, England, (seventeenth century).

Piece of Catlinite, roughly blocked in form of pipe by Indians. Found at the Great Red Pipestone Quarry in Minnesota, thirty years ago.

Two old English pipe-bowls found in an Indian grave, Lancaster county, Pa.

Corncobs from ancient Pueblo ruins in Utah. One showing grains of corn.

Eleven arrow-heads from New Jersey.

Two white quartz arrow-heads from Chester county, Pa.

One flint point from San Miguel Island, California.

Fractured pebbles from the Haldeman Rock Retreat at Chickis, Lancaster county, Pa.

Seventy pamphlets on archæological, philological and ethnological subjects.

Dr. Brinton mentioned the recent sale to parties in Europe, of the library of the late Abbe Brasseur de Bourbourg, as increased by M. Pinard. In many respects this was one of the most valuable collections in existence of books and manuscripts on American archæology and linguistics, and Dr. Brinton stigmatized it as a discredit to this country that such a library had not found purchasers in the United States.

Messrs. D. G. Brinton and Henry Phillips, Jr., were appointed delegates to represent the Society at the approaching Congress of Americanists, to be held at Copenhagen in the coming autumn.

The new 5-cent piece was laid before the Society, and it was resolved that the Society was gratified to observe the improvement of the coinage of the United States as exhibited thereon.

Mr. Edwin Atlee Barber, from the Committee on Archæology, reported that the removal of the Society's archæological possessions from the Hall of the Society, would not be advisable at the present time.

A communication was read from Mr. Horatio Hale, of Ontario, Canada, a corresponding member of the Society, on "The Poetry and Songs of the North American Indians," after which a discussion ensued on the morals and manners of the Indians, and their capacity for civilization.

Mr. Charles Henry Hart, the Historiographer, announced the death of Charles Perrin Smith, of Trenton, N. J., a corresponding member of the Society, which took place on January 27, 1883, in his sixty-fourth year.

March 1st.

Among the donations received at this meeting were several rare coins of the short-lived Roman and Venetian Republics of 1849.

Mr. Horatio Hale read a paper on the migrations of the Amerian Indians, as evidenced by language, which was followed by a discussion on the subject. Attention was called to the alleged discovery of prehistoric maps or plans in Switzerland, inscribed on stones with marks and dots.

Rev. John P. Lundy made a communication upon a remarkable fact which he had just discovered after long study, viz., that the Mongolian symbolism of writing was to be found on the rock sculptures of Mexico and Central America, and that by the aid of the former the latter could be readily and easily deciphered; that these latter were evidently of Mongolian origin, and that he had interpreted some of the symbols in Stephens' *Yucatan* by means of Mongolian symbols. Dr. Lundy, in announcing his discovery, stated he would go fully into the subject at the next meeting of the Society.

Dr. Brinton read a paper on the recent European contributions to the study of American Archæology, in which he passed high eulogy upon the recent labors of Professor Leon de Rosny, the Comte de Charency, Dr. Hamy, the Marquis de Nadaillac, and others. This paper has been printed.

April 5th.

Mr. Henry Phillips, Jr., read an account of recent discoveries near the river Euphrates.

Rev. John P. Lundy read an essay upon the celebrated Dighton Rock inscription, which he had translated by means of Chinese radicals, to the following effect:

"A chain or band of folk from the sunrising (or East), after a long and stormy voyage, found the harbor of a great island. It was wild, uninhabited, green and fruitful. On landing and tying up our boats, we first gave thanks and adoration to God, Shang-Ti, the Supreme Ruler of the universe. We then sacrificed a human head to the moon, burning it and the body on a round sun-altar. The next morning a bright sun shone auspiciously on all things below; the heavenly omens and prognostics, duly consulted, were all favorable. We then struck across the tangled forest-land westward. Our mouths hankered after something to eat and drink. We found the blue-black maize of our native land and wild fruit. We filled our rice-kettles. We dug a pit under the rocks of a hill-side, put in our corn and fruit, and cooked them. We sat down under the shady trees, covered with wild grapes, and ate our fill. When the moon rose, we retired to our hut or bough-house, and slept. The next day we pushed on westward through the tangle, guided by the sun.

The chief gave the orders and led the way. We all followed in close march. We crossed some low hills and came to green meadows, filled with wild rice or oats. A stream of water came down from the hills. We stopped; we made a great feast; we sang and danced around our big kettle; its sweet odors curled up high to Shang-Ti, our God and Father in heaven. This memorial-stone or altar is dedicated to Shang-Ti, our Ruler and Guide to this newly-found island."

Mr. Outerbridge called to the attention of the Society, a novel conjecture as to the manner in which the hieroglyphs were engraved on the obelisk. Mr. Chandler exhibited an antique ring from the ruins of Carthage, on which was engraved a remarkable animal, something between an elk and a rhinoceros. Mr. Myer exhibited the Penn Bi-Centennial medal in brass.

Mr. Charles Henry Hart, the Historiographer, announced the death of Lucius Quintius Cincinnatus Elmer, a corresponding member of the Society, as having taken place at his home, Bridgeton, N. J., on March 11th, in the ninety-first year of his age.

A communication was read from Alfred Sharpless, of West Chester, in relation to collections of American archæology formed by himself from relics found in Chester, Delaware and Lancaster counties. But very few burial-places were found in the section of country examined, and these were mostly modern. Very few caves and no human-made mounds have been found in Chester county. The camping-grounds of the Indians were generally sharply defined by the débris left behind them. They were invariably near a spring of good water, and on ground sufficiently elevated to be out of the reach of floods and freshets. He spoke of the old "Indian trail" from the Delaware to the Susquehanna, and of the island near Peach Bottom, on the latter river, known as "Caldwell's Island," formerly a favorite camping-ground of the aborigines. The slate-stone of the vicinity furnished the material for making their implements and weapons. Three or four miles south of this island, at a point known as Bald Friars, there are some sculptured rocks, on which the markings are still quite plain, and are evidently of very ancient origin, and apparently historical in character. Steatite quarries are also in the neighborhood.

May 3d.

Mr. W. S. Baker exhibited a very fine Washington medal, of which only two are known to exist. It bears on the obverse a full-face bust, with the inscription, "First in war, first in peace, first in the hearts of his countrymen," and underneath the name "George Washington." On the reverse, "In remembrance of the Centennial, July 4, 1876," above a view of Independence Hall; exergue, "Independence Hall as in 1776." The medal is said to be of English origin.

Mr. E. A. Barber exhibited some antique Japanese tobacco pipes, which he had recently received as a gift from the Imperial University of Tokio. Among the collection are several very curious examples of the early part of the seventeenth century, which are amongst the earliest Japanese pipes made. Some of them have twisted stems; others are beautifully engraved, and all of them are made of metal,—nickel, silver, iron, brass, or bronze.

A letter was read from the physician at the Round Valley Agency, Civelo, California, giving an account of the native tribes in that vicinity, of which he writes, there are seven, entirely distinct in customs, languages, ceremonies, and traditional history. Among them there is something of a church organization, to which only the most prominent members of the tribe are admitted, and all their traditional history and knowledge are preserved sacred within this narrow circle from outsiders. Those Indians who do not belong to the "Sweat-house," know nothing of their traditions.

A communication was read from Señor Chazara, of Tlacitaplan, Mexico, offering to send the Society accounts of aboriginal antiquities and customs.

Mr. Henry Phillips, Jr., read an account of the finding of a hoard of Roman coins near Cremona, Italy, on the 5th of last February.

A communication was read from Mr. John Deans, of Vancouver's Island, British Columbia, a corresponding member of the Society, on the Haidah Indians of Queen Charlotte's Islands.

It is not the custom of the Society to hold meetings during the summer months, and therefore the next meeting was not held till

October 4th.

At this meeting a large number of donations were placed before the Society, among which were an interesting collection of coins, catalogued and arranged in a handsome cabinet, from Dr. and Mrs. Kingston Goddard; and a wooden pipe, representing a grotesque head, from Señor Don Vicente Fernandez, of Mexico. Dr. Brinton, from the delegation appointed by the Society to attend the Congres des Americanistes at Copenhagen in August, gave an account of the events that had taken place there, and described several valuable collections of American antiquities seen by him at Hamburg and Cologne. Professor H. Carvill Lewis, presented a "natural" palæolithic implement from Chester county, Pa., which so closely resembled an artificial production, as easily to be mistaken for one, and spoke of the error into which archæologists have often fallen on that account.

Mr. Isaac Myer exhibited an intaglio copy and impressions in wax of an antique seal, two-thirds of an inch long by half an inch wide, the size of a small thumb-nail, on which was engraved with great beauty, a horse and fifteen full-length figures. He described the original as known in Europe as the seal of Michael Angelo, and that it is said to have been engraved on sard by Pyrogeteles, of the time of Alexander the Great, (circa 300 B. C.) He also showed a copper-plate engraving of the same, greatly enlarged, to be found in the *Gentleman's Magazine* for 1751.

The Treasurer reported that the Hall of the Society had been leased to it for another year, from November 1, 1883, at the same rent.

Mr. Charles Henry Hart, the Historiographer, announced the death of the Hon. George Sharswood, late Chief Justice of the Supreme Court of Pennsylvania, an honorary member of the Society, who died in this city, May 28, 1883, in his seventy-third year.

Mr. Edwin A. Barber, exhibited an antique iron pipe, lately sent him from Zurich, which had been found with some Roman remains of the second century. But the pipe itself is evidently a Dutch pipe of the seventeenth century.

The following communication was read from Dr. Macedo, of Lima, Peru, on the aborigines of that country, their history and customs, presenting some new views.

"At the present date, two small collections of Peruvian antiquities only can be found in Lima. One is owned by Don Nicolas Sanz, and the other by Don Manuel Espantoso. Both contain from 800 to 1000 pieces of pottery, among which, according to my estimate, about 20 per cent. are of great value, the remainder being little above ordinary.

In the neighborhood of Lima, the Port of Ancon, which is situated about eighteen miles to the northeast, is the locality where the most important specimens in cloth, silver, gold, copper, wooden instruments and mummies have beon discovered. The jars in this place are of common clay, and the idols of mud or of wood. A good idea may be had of the excavations made at Ancon, prosecuted by Messrs. W. Reiss and A. Stube, who have published five volumes, under the title of "Peruvian Antiquities; the Necropolis of Ancon in Peru." Judging Ancon from its cemeteries, it must have been a populous city. The cloth from this place is so varied and fine, and with such varied colors, that some of it, although more than four hundred (400) years under ground, seems to have been manufactured at the present day, such is the freshness of its tints, particularly the red, black and yellow. The articles of which the high colors are most conspicuous, are those which the Indians called Uncuñas, a kind of small handkerchief in which the women kept the coca, also the CHUSPAS, a sort of bag with braces, in which the Indians used to prepare their choice coca. The cloth varies according to the use to be made of it. Some specimens are CHUCOS, a kind of shirt without sleeves, which was the garment used by the Indians; it is adorned with idols, birds and triangular figures. Another variety looks like net or crochet lace in the form of a shawl, and still another fabric ornamented with two-faced idols of different colors. The weaving is so even and close that it looks like poplin. Two horizontal posts were stuck in the ground which the Indians call FACARPUS; horizontal threads were stretched along and across the piece to be woven: in the centre was a species of weaver's reed which they called MAGUA, the object of which was to pack the horizontal threads up or down in order to cross the texture. The thread for weaving was rolled up on a sort of wooden spool. To tighten the texture, a small bone instrument with a sharp point was employed, which was called HUICHUNA. With this simple and rudimentary apparatus they were able to leave us the relics which are now found. During the long years I have spent in antiquarian researches, I have not been able to obtain cloth like that of Ancon. Specimens in silver and gold have been also excavated in abundance from this place, and it is surprising that the Incas, without being acquainted with the use of cylinders, have been able to laminate some metals to the consistency of paper, sometimes representing idols, ornaments for dresses or vases, girdles and animals. Light silver vases with double base have been found and it is impossible to tell where the joining is made. The wooden idols are rough and imperfect, but as the Incas knew nothing of the use of iron or steel, it is easy to understand that having no instruments to overcome the woody fibre, they could not leave us any notable works of this material. We may also notice that the tints for dying their colors were extracted only from the vegetable kingdom.

The Incas were buried in a sitting posture, with their garments, utensils and some food, such as Indian corn, beans and chicha acca, a kind of sweet liquor; showing that they believed in a voyage to another and distant country after death.

Instruments of Agriculture.

There were principally three. The FACUA; a curved stick, more than a yard long, with a point at one end, and a curved handle at the other, and a cross piece like a stirrup at a certain distance from the pointed end where the force was applied by the right foot to send the point into the ground to raise a clod of it which they called CHAMPA. Four, six or eight Indians in file performed this labor.

RAUCANA. A hand implement of wood, strong and curved to an angle at one of its extremities, which is pointed; the other is round for the hand. The use is to remove the ground.

PALETA. A cylindrical wooden instrument ending in a kind of platter of semi-circular shape, used to till the ground.

Arms.

HUARACA. The sling and arrows were the only arms used against the enemy at a distance. The former was made of hemp, cotton and wool, of long strands strongly twisted, with an opening at the centre about a third of a yard long, sunk in the middle. The stone was placed there, and after being repeatedly whirled around, it was discharged by letting loose one of the sides of the sling held by the little finger of the right hand by a sort of loop attached to it.

The ARROWS. The bows and arrows were of the usual shape, but the points of the arrows instead of being of chipped silica, like those of the Mexicans, were some pointed and toothed on either side, some shaped like a lance, and others round and sharp-pointed; all were made of a black vitreous wood called by the Indians, *Chonta*. The shaft was made of a very light stick, surrounded at the extremity by two feather fringes. There are also some arrows terminating in a little ball, which must have been used to hunt birds.

The MACANA. This implement consists of a spherical stone with a hole through the centre to attach it to the extremity of a strong wooden handle. These clubs are of different forms and material, some being of copper and others of stone. The copper ones are the most varied, some being in the shape of stars with sharp points; others spherical, edged with spirals, others plain and of an oval form. The greatest number of stone specimens are spherical. The Lances and picks are very long and made of a kind of hard polished wood called *Chonta*. These of course were for close combats.

MUSICAL INSTRUMENTS.

The QUENA is an instrument half a yard long, made of a hollow reed, cylindrical in shape, like a flute, with six notes in the front, one note in the back, and a mouth-piece with a small notch; it produces melancholy sounds and is accompanied by, contralto. In the interior of Peru, it is played upon by the Indians even at the present time, generally late at night. The tunes they play are called *Tristes* or *Yaravies*.

The PINQUILLO is a small flute made of thin bones of animals, with four holes and a mouth-piece. It produces very high sounds. It is an instrument used by shepherds.

The SICO is an instrument consisting of a series of pipes made of hollow reeds, diminishing in size and bound by two wooden flat pieces, one in front and the other behind, twisted with thread that binds all the pipes like an organ. It produces grave and acute sounds, and the Indians of the Andes make use of this instrument in their dances, which they call *Ayarachis*.

The HUANCAR is a small drum, or a hollow wooden box, whose ends are covered with a piece of vellum or skin well tanned. Before the Huancas were conquered by the Incas, they used for their drum-heads, the tanned skin of their enemies.

The PUTUTU is an instrument made of clay, sometimes in the shape of a snail, others in circular and crooked pipes, and some are made even of the snail itself. It requires a good deal of strength to get out of it a grave and loud sound. It doubtless was employed as a War Trumpet. The Morochucos Indians now make use of it to bring in the wild cattle and to drive the bulls to the localities where they are to fight. Some of these Pututus made of bull-horns have proved to be very effective.

Dress Materials.

The wool of the Vicuña, Llama, Alpaca and the sheep and also cotton were employed in the fabrication of dresses. Vicuña wool, as the choicest, was reserved for the sole use of the Inca and royal family, whose garments were woven by the Virgins of the Sun. The Imperial insignia was the LLAUTU, of a crimson color, the fringe falling over the face and placed as a diadem around the head. The Crown Princes also wore the Llautu of a yellow color, but without any fringe. The cotton fabrics were used by the natives of the east or warm climates; those of the colder climates wore garments of sheep's wool. Llama wool was used to make ropes called *Huasca*, and also large bags.

The Emperor carried a wooden sceptre with gold and silver ornaments, gold earrings, gold knee-buckles and bracelets, with sandals of hemp. The UNCO was a sort of frock without sleeves, with allegorical designs.

Food.

The Indian corn, potatoes, wheat, beans, hulluco, quinua and havas, were the principal productions. From the corn or Sara, the Indians made and still continue to make, a sort of fermented liquor, Acca, which was greatly esteemed by the Incas. From the same grain they made the bread for the feasts of Ragmy, whom they called Zancu; it was kneaded by the Virgins consecrated to the Sun.

Writing.

The Incas were unacquainted with any system of writing by means of letters or of hieroglyphics, but availed themselves of the Quipus or system of knotted strings, to transmit their principal dates of peace or war, the statistics of marriage, death, distribution of land, taxes and labors of their subjects. The Quipucamayoes were charged with its management. The Quipus consisted of a series of strings of different colors, as red, white, black, coffee color and yellow; others of combined colors, and all were attached at the top to a thick cord. In these threads are to be seen knots differing in form and distance, and sometimes a series of knots surrounding a larger one. Many historians believe that this system is applicable only to numerical figures of addition and subtraction. But a passage in the work of Ollanta, page 108, states that the Inca Inpanquis received a dispatch in a bundle of Quipus, which was deciphered by the Astrologer, a Sage Amauta, to the effect that the black knot indi ated that Ollanta had been burnt, and the three knots lying together near a fifth one revealed that the Province of Antis was already captured, and in the power of the king; consequently this passage shows that by means of the Quipus, facts have been disclosed, and that if long and complete sentences could not be read on them, at least they furnish more complicated ideas than those of mere addition or subtraction. Although the Aztec civilization in Mexico was contemporary with that of the Incas, we have every reason to believe that the Empires progressed without contact with each other. Their system of conquest, their writing, their architecture, their laws, their utensils and instruments prove this truth. While the Aztec civilization in Mexico or Anahuac extended itself by force and bloody wars, the Incas conquered by persuasion and paternal laws. The Aztecs sacrificed hundreds of prisoners to their divinities; the Incas honored the Sun by sacrificing lambs and llamas. The Aztecs have left us their history by means of hieroglyphics; the Incas by means of their Quipus, architecture, utensils and manner of burial. All were different. In every important locality under the rule of the Incas, may be found in the tombs, Huacos or jars, as well as other utensils, but it is beyond doubt that the best place for these researches was to the north of our present Capital, through the whole extent of the five provinces, which before the conquest of the Inca Inpanqui, son of Pacha-Cutec, were under the domination of the great Chimu. These provinces are Paramonga, Huarmey, Santa, Guañape and Chimu. Near Trujillo are yet to be seen the ruins of the Palace of the Curaca, Gran Chimu. The most noted and thoroughly explored Huacos at present in that region are those of Carma Samanco, Chimbote, Chepen, Nepeña, Caja-marca and Trujillo; the clay of which these jars or Huacos were made was generally a light red, seldom black, but very fine and light in weight. The mouldings, as correct in the heads as in their anatomical proportions and expressions, equal those wrought by the chisel of the Renaissance, but it is not so with the proportions of the body and the extremities, which are imperfect and deformed. In this great variety of pottery may be found all sorts of allegorical and mythological groups; reproductions of animals known by them as leopards, llamas, vicuñas, dogs, foxes, bats, crabs, serpents, many kinds of fishes, and birds, as well as fruits; a Penal System similar to the punishment of the Tarpeian Rock; cutaneous diseases even are represented; warriors in their coats of mail, armed with their Macanos, dancing figures, fortresses, figures disguised with faces of animals, Satyrs, Indian corn and fruits; Genii with large wings, human bodies with condor's head, others representing a serpent with human feet and hands, armed with darts and shields; idols in silver, gold, wood, copper and cloth. All of these archæological riches, or at least three quarters of the private collections, have been dug up in the ancient domain of the Gran Chimu.

It is difficult to decide, if all of the above have been produced before the conquest of the Inca Inpanqui, son of the ninth Emperor of the Incas, or whether the Gran Chimu Indians arrived at this advancement during Jahuantinsuyo's Empire.

I shall venture to give my opinion based on the following facts:

First: The predominating idea of the Gran Chimu was the love, and even idolatry, of all natural objects which could have any influence on the welfare of the people. This of itself afforded abundant material for reproduction, whilst on the other hand, during Manco Capac's Empire, from its foundation, no other Supreme Being was known but the Sun as their visible, and Pachacamac as their invisible divinity, strictly forbidding all other idolatry.

Second: In Cuzco, the capital of the Inca Empire, and in all the places inhabited by savage and wandering Indians, within any civilization anterior to the laws given by the Incas, the variety of reproductions in clay, above mentioned, are not to be found in any of their tombs.

Third: The Incas or inhabitants of the coast like those of the Gran Chimu, on account of the warm climate, have a fantastic and creative imagination, not as with the race of Aymaraos and Huancas, who, living in colder climates on the other side of the Andes, possess active imagination, though more suitable for reasoning and for strength of mind. For these reasons, I am inclined to believe that the richness and variety of the pottery of the Gran Chimu existed before the influence of the Inca civilization was felt.

In the Department of Ancash, north of Lima, in a place called Recuay, which is six leagues north-east of the capitol, Huaraz, Mr. Icaza, a planter and miner of said place, after four years of excavating, formed a collection of 160 jars or Huacos of special and important significance. All of these are of very fine white and red clay, the general form being spherical, with black and red figures. The animals mostly portrayed are serpents, dragons and fantastical creatures with huge claws, and jaws like those of a crocodile, but the most important thing to be observed is the strong resemblance of the faces, which have a large, straight nose, large mouth and thin lips. This physiognomy is so uniform, that after looking at one, all the rest appear made from the same type and in such uniform manner that it is impossible to confound them with the faces of the other pottery of the Inca Empire. The same thing applies to the painted red and black ornaments. This would induce one to think that the pre-Incarial civilization of this place kept it isolated and independent until the close of that Empire. In this rich collection, which is also now in Berlin forming part of mine, there is a jar which represents an Indian extended and bound, whose bowels are being devoured by two vultures, which recalls the fable of Prometheus in the Greek mythology. Another bears a god Priapus with all the emblems of fecundity, and surrounded by women who implore his protection. There are also Zaramas, war councils, fortresses, dancing figures with Llamas, warriors with shield in hand, Incas seated upon their thrones, etc.

PACHACAMAC, or the dominions of CUYSMANCUS CURACA, before Inca

Ii.panqui's conquest, is nine leagues south of Lima, where the ruins of its palaces are yet to be found. Neither from the cemeteries in this locality nor in the excavations which have been made, has it been possible to obtain any valuable objects. Many mummies, *Chuas* or small dishes of clay, ornaments, fine designs of jars and instruments of labor and several varieties of cloth; these are all that have yet been found. I make this statement in order to prove that the ceramics reflect the ideas of a country. There they adored only an invisible god, Pachacamac, and a visible idol, Rimac, by which interpreter they offered their prayers to their creator; with this elevated idea of Divine unity, their pottery could be but ordinary utensils.

From Cuzco, which was the Empire's former capital, I have some Huacos, cloth and various utensils, although but few of any value; some stone mortars well wrought, a few common jars and an Unco sleeveless frock have been the sole fruit of my efforts. Two causes explain the scarcity of the Huacos there:

First: Adoring only the sun with prohibition of any other kind of idolatry, the Huaco-makers mostly employed themselves in manufacturing ordinary ware, such as jars, *Chuas* or dishes, and jars or pots, rather than in representing mythological or allegorical ideas.

Second: Retaining even to the present day great veneration and respect for the relics of their forefathers, the Indians do not permit the excavation of their tombs; and only on Good Friday, through a kind of superstition, it has become permissible to open their burial places. So difficult is it to form a good collection in Cuzco, that in the catalogue published by Mme. Centeno, a respectable lady of that city,—amid a quantity of pots, Chuas or jars, there are scarcely twenty-five of any historical importance. Mr. Montes, who also proposed to form a collection in Cuzco, could only obtain at a great price, silver, gold and stone specimens, but of pottery, which is the most important for history, he could obtain very few relics.

In my opinion, the great Chimu burial places are those which contain and have yielded the most important treasures to the Incas archæology."

November 1st.

Vice-President Brinton in the chair. Among the donations were a series of mediæval coins of various towns of the famous Hansa League, presented by Mr Sophus A. Bergsoë, of Copenhagen; also some antique Greek and Roman coins from Mr. A. E. Richards, of Florence. The Government of Victoria presented Brough-Smith's great work on the Australian aborigines.

A valuable present of Peruvian pottery was received from Hon. Walton W. Evans, of New Rochelle, N Y., to whom an especial vote of thanks was directed to be returned. Hon. Washington Townsend presented a package of Confederate and colonial paper money. Mr. Phillips exhibited tracings of two interesting maps of America, of a date early in the sixteenth century, from the Royal Library at Stockholm.

A communication was read from Dr. Melesio Medal, of Patzcuaro, Mexico, inclosing a drawing and description of some early Mexican hieroglyphics in a church at that place.

The hieroglyphics, which were discovered by Dr. Medal in the tower of the Church of Tazacuaro, a small island in the lake of Patzcuaro, inhabited solely by Indians, are thought by the curè, Mr. Arcenio Robledo, to have been invented by the Archbishop Vasco di Quiroga, in order to disseminate the true faith among the natives. According to his ideas the meaning is as follows:—

First figure—In a parallelogram a cross with the initial M on the right (Maria) and J (Jesus) on the left, but according to Dr. Medal's opinion, in which he is sustained by the drawing which accompanied his letter, the M should be on the left and the J on the right. On the right of the figure and outside is the full disk of the sun with a human face, surrounded by rays; on the left, outside, is the crescent moon. In the lower right hand corner of the parallelogram, below the cross, is a figure like a nail or spike, probably referring to the Crucifixion.

Second figure—A star on the left, and a pair of crossed keys on the right of an eagle on a cactus, holding in his beak and talon a serpent.

In many places in this vicinity there are a number of small mounds of earth and flat stones, known as Vacatos, which according to ancient traditions are looked upon as being tombs of Indian families. In these are often found all manners of odd objects, utensils, images, etc.

Mr. W. S. Baker exhibited the Temple medal to be given by the Pennsylvania Academy of the Fine Arts as a prize. The dies were made by Mr. George T. Morgan and the excellence of the workmanship was especially commented on.

A communication was read from Mr. James Deans, of Vancouver's Island, accompanying a photograph of one of the remarkable Chinese coins lately found near there in a deep digging far below the surface of the earth. The best information which he could procure led him to believe it a calendar issued about 2600 B. C.

Mr. Hart exhibited autographs of Gilbert Stuart, the Scotch antiquary, and Gilbert Stuart, the American artist, and commented on a supposed similarity in their handwritings.

Mr. Hart read a memoir of the late Hon. James Madison Porter, of Easton, Pa., which he had prepared, by request, for the New England Historic Genealogical Society Memorial Biographies.

The attention of the Society was called to the wants and merits of the Archæological Institute of America; and also to the new journal of East Indian Folklore, edited at Ambala by Captain Richard Temple, entitled *Punjaub Queries*.

Dr. Brinton made some remarks on the good work lately done by the Bureau of Ethnology, especially referring to their investigations into American sign language, through the means of which the American rock inscriptions can be easily read. He stated that the sign language can be divided into three centres which agree with the same divisions of rock inscriptions:—

1. The Algonkin, which extends from the Atlantic Ocean to beyond the Rocky Monntains.
2. The New Mexican.
3. The Navajo, which are also found in British America.

By means of the rock centre theory, inscriptions in the Esquimaux tongue two centuries old have been truly deciphered.

Dr. Brinton also spoke of the great works on the Klamath and Omaha languages, which in about two years will be ready, and referred to the peculiar advantages under which they were studied.

Mr. Philip H. Law was requested to read at the March meeting a paper on "Secret Societies, as preservative of rites, laws, and customs."

Vice-President Brinton was requested to deliver the annual address in January, 1884.

Messrs. Hart, Davis, and Baker were appointed a Committee to nominate officers, etc., for 1884.

DECEMBER 6TH.

Mr. John R. Baker exhibited a very fine uncirculated specimen of the so-called "subsidy money," being a thaler struck in 1778 by the Landgrave of Hesse, from the silver which had been paid him by the British Government for the soldiers sold by him to fight against the American Colonists. The coin is not common, and in this uncirculated condition is believed to be unique.

Mr. Barber, Curator of Antiquities, presented the following report on the accessions to the Society's cabinet:

"During the past year the increased interest and activity of the members of the Society have been productive of gratifying results. Through individual exertions, several valuable additions have been made to the cabinet of antiquities. The circular which was ordered to be printed for distribution amongst societies and scientific gentlemen abroad, has been the means of materially increasing the number of objects of archæological interest, and it may now be safely said that the experiment has proved successful, even beyond expectation. Many correspondents in Central and South America have expressed their intention of forwarding to the Society, at the earliest opportunity, rare and valuable collections of antiquities, of which they are now in possession.

Amongst the donations received during the year, the following are worthy of notice: Flint arrow-heads from the ancient burial places of California; white quartz specimens from Chester County, Pa., and a series of slate points from the shell-heaps of New Jersey. The collections of pottery include some fine pieces of painted and lustred ware, from the prehistoric pueblos of Utah, and ornamented fragments of earthenware from Pennsylvania and New Jersey. Amongst the ancient Pueblo pottery are some corrugated specimens, which show the process of manufacture. The vessels, of which the broken pieces originally formed a part, were built up by coiling long strips of clay spirally, a process employed by many of the American tribes. The exterior surface was ornamented by means of the corner of a right angled flat stone, or stick which was pressed into the plastic clay at regular intervals along the successive bands, each row of incisions breaking joints with the one above. The indentations were then finished by the pressure of the thumb, as is shown by the fine lines of the cuticle which have left very distinct impressions. The effect of this style of ornamentation (which is characteristic of much of the ancient Pueblo ware) is quite artistic. Sometimes two or three bands have been left unornamented, which heightens the effect, and relieves the monotony of the scale-like appearance of the surface. The painted specimens are generally ornamented with geometrical devices in black, on a white ground.

A collection of corn-cobs from these same ruined buildings possesses particular interest. They vary from three to five inches in length, some of them showing grains of the yellow maize which still adhere to them. They were found mostly amongst the *debris* on the floors of the ruins; some were extracted from the mortar of the walls, where they had been imbedded by the architects centuries ago.

A series of specimens of *catlinite*, from the Great Red Pipestone Quarry, in Minnesota, shows the different varieties of that celebrated stone, which has been used for many generations by the Indian tribes of North America, in the manufacture of tobacco-pipes. Pieces of the finest quality, most highly prized by the natives, are from the centre of the vein, being characterized by a beautiful deep red color, mottled thickly with pink spots. Other fragments are of a light buff or rich cream color, whilst still others are flesh-colored on one side and dark slate on the other. The most interesting specimen in the collection is an L-shaped piece, from the purest portion of the layer. It has been roughly cut into the form of a pipe, and was found, upwards of thirty years ago, in the *debris* of the quarry, where it had evidently been dropped, before being finished, by some native pipe-maker.

A number of early British clay pipes (probably belonging to the seventeenth century) from the vicinity of London, England, possess considerable interest. The bowls are of small size, some of them possessing the marks or initials of their makers on the flat heels. Two similar examples, of probably later date, were found in Indian graves in Lancaster County, Pa. The latter were brought to this country by early English settlers and traded to the Indians.

Señor Don Vicente Fernandez has sent to the Society, a curious tobacco pipe, which is said to have been dug up near Guanajuato, Mexico. It is made of wood, and carved to represent a human head—evidently a caricature or likeness of some particular person. The absence of an eye, the twisted nose and bloated cheeks suggest the possibility of portraiture. The bowl lies in the back of the head, while the stem-hole passes through the neck. The illustration which accompanies this (having been kindly furnished by *Our Continent* Publishing Co.*), will give some idea of this curious relic. Some doubt exists, however, as to the antiquity of this object. The sharply-cut spiral of the stem orifice, and the striking resemblance of the head to certain representations of Punchinello with cocked hat, strongly indicate a Spanish source. The very fresh appearance of the carving seems to point to a recent origin, possibly not antedating the last century.

FIG. 1.

WOODEN PIPE, FROM MEXICO.
Presented by Sr. Vicente Fernandez.

From Mr. James Deans of Victoria, British Columbia, the Society has received some specimens of *Hiaqua* shells (a species of *Dentalium* or natural wampum) long, slender tubes, obtained by the natives at a great depth, off Cape Flattery. The tribes of the northwest coast used these extensively as a circulating medium, the value being in a geometrical proportion to the length. A string of forty shells to the fathom, was worth nearly twice as much as a string of fifty to the fathom. The Indians of Vancouver Island, Washington Territory and Oregon, have used these shells as a standard of value for many generations. The specimens presented by Mr. Deans were found on Vancouver Island beneath the branches of a tree, in which the body of a child had been placed, as is the mortuary custom of some tribes. The burial-case having rotted away, the remains were precipitated to the ground.

---

* From an article entitled *Native American Caricature*, by E. A. Barber. Vol. IV. No 86.

Amongst the tribes on the northwest coast of British Columbia and Alaska a copper plate currency was used. The Haidah Indians of Queen Charlotte's Islands, British Columbia, employ these copper plates as a circulating medium to this day. They are made of pure native copper which is found near the junction of Alaska and British Columbia. The plates are beaten out rudely with stone hammers and some of them are very old. They are called *Thucahs* by the Indians. Mr. Deans informs me that plates of this kind were worth, in 1869, from $250 to $500 each. He saw one chief in the possession of 25 or 30 of them which he valued at several thousand dollars. They measure from 18 inches to two feet in length,—a coin obviously inconvenient to handle or use as a pocket piece.

FIG. 2.

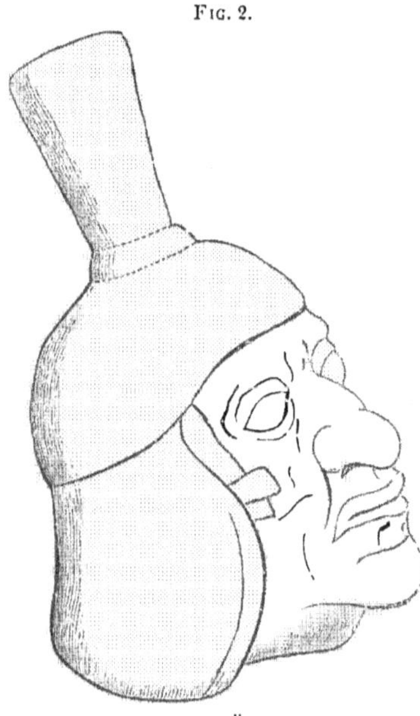

ANCIENT PERUVIAN "PORTRAIT VASE."
Presented by Hon. Walton W. Evans.

A Peruvian musical instrument, resembling a flageolet, has been received from the Hon. Walton W. Evans of New Rochelle, N. Y. The material is cane, such instruments being still in use by some of the mountain tribes of Peru. The Society has also received from the same gentleman, a valuable collection of ancient Peruvian vases, which were brought by him from Peru about thirty years ago. They were taken from an extensive burial-ground, which extended for about twenty miles along the coast, near the mouth of the Santa River. Some of these are superb examples of the noted *portrait vases*, which were drinking vessels moulded in the form of human heads. probably after individual models. Others are of the syphon form,—globular bottles surmounted by arched tubes terminating in a straight spout. Some of them are decorated with paintings of animals, and others have mouldings in relief of monkeys, owls and men. In this collection is an old Pueblo meal jar from Laguna, New Mexico. This measures about twelve inches in diameter, and shows traces of long use. It is particularly valuable on account of its peculiar ornamentation. The surface is decorated with conventionalized paintings of serpents, which, we are informed by Rev. John Menaul, a missionary who has spent many years with the Pueblo Indians of New Mexico, possess some symbolical significance, which, at this day, is understood only by the medicine men or priests of the tribe.

Fig. 3.

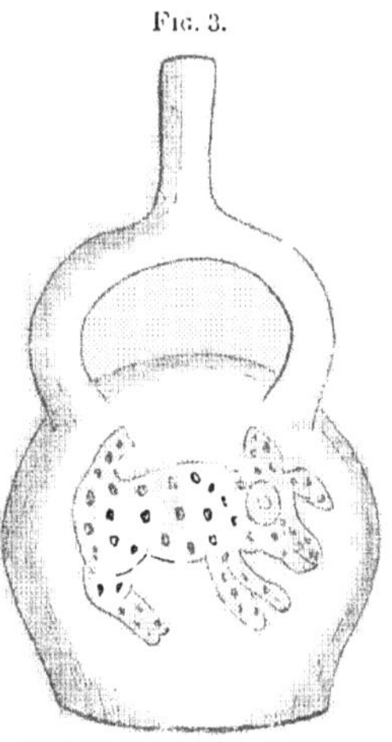

PERUVIAN WATER BOTTLE.
From Hon. W. W. Evans.

A number of Colonial and Confederate notes have been received from the Hon. Washington Townsend, of West Chester, Pa., and will shortly be framed and exhibited in the Society's room.

Amongst other prospective donations, the Society has been promised some large stone idols from Nicaragua, and several valuable acquisitions to the cabinet may be expected at an early day from Mexico and Peru. A new set of label cards has been procured for the cabinet, and it is believed that in a short time our case room will have become exhausted. Under such circumstances it will be found necessary to increase the number of cases, when their character and arrangement may be changed."

In the discussion upon the report which ensued, Dr Brinton stated that he believed he had made an important discovery in American Ethnology which he would soon make public.

Fig. 4.

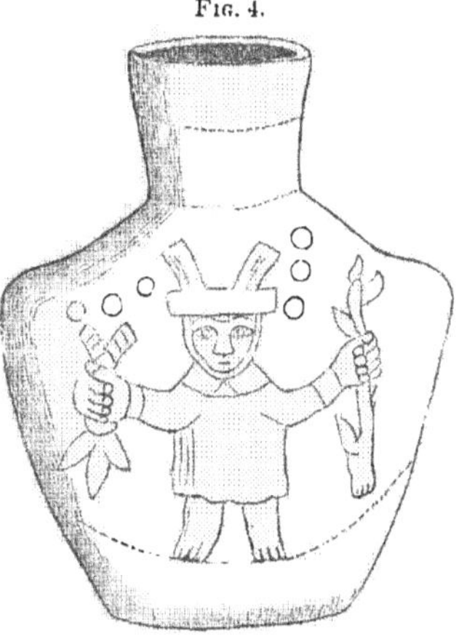

PERUVIAN JAR, WITH ORNAMENTATION IN LOW RELIEF.
From Hon. W. W. Evans.

Mr. Henry Phillips, Jr., exhibited a valuable manuscript, being the journal of William Sullivan, a private in the British army, who served in America from 1775 to 1778, embracing accounts of the marches, battles, sieges, campaigns, and cities occupied by the British troops during that period. It is a 12mo. of 422 pp., beautifully and clearly printed by the pen in letters simulating type, so that the effect is that of a printed book. It contains muster rolls and maps and descriptions of cities, as well as the personal experiences of the writer.

Among the battles narrated, are those of Bunker's Hill, the siege of Boston, Red Bank, Germantown, Long Island, Monmouth, Trenton, the Brandywine, etc. He makes mention of the Conway and Kitwallader (*sic*) duel. The preface is dated Philadelphia, April 22, 1778.

Mr. Sullivan, who appears to have been a man of education, showed his good sense by marrying an American woman, deserting as soon as he could from the invading army, and settled down to become a citizen of the United States.

An especial vote of thanks was tendered by the Society to Mr. J. Hays Carson, who desired to retire from the Recording Secretaryship after long and faithful services.

Dr. Brinton, presented a new work entitled a *Manual of American Aboriginal Literature*, being an amplification of an address by himself, before the Congres des Americanistes, at Copenhagen, this summer.

Mr. Hart, called the attention of the Society to an article, in the last number of the *Magazine of American History*, upon a supposed Aztec coin.

The committee to effect an insurance upon the Society's property at the Hall, was ordered to do so at once, and draw on the Treasurer for the amount.

Rev. J. F. Garrison, mentioned the existence of a manuscript journal, kept by a member of his family two years before the Revolution, and spoke of the singular freedom of manners, etc., which it evinced.

The annual election for officers and committees was held, and a number of resident members were also elected.

The Secretary, whilst congratulating the Society upon its continued prosperity, would respectfully call at the same time to the attention of its members, the necessity for a considerable increase in its permanent funds, for the purpose of obtaining a larger hall, where its property could be more accessible and better displayed, and also for the more frequent issue of the Report of its proceedings, which in that case could be made much more full than at present. The life of a Society lies in its publications, and a stimulus to literary effort, that is now lacking, would be given to our members by the knowledge that their papers, if worthy of diffusion, would be presented by us to the Archæological world. There is no

Society in this section of the country that occupies the field in which we have labored for the past quarter century, yet our endeavors are not appreciated by this community, as they deserve to be, however, much outside of our own city we have received a proper and merited recognition. Our ranks although wonderfully increased are far from full; our exchequer, while sufficing for our modest wants, does not permit us to be of that full value to Science which we could readily be.

All which is respectfully submitted, by

HENRY PHILLIPS, Jr.
Corresponding Secretary and Treasurer.

PHILADELPHIA, December 31st, 1883

NECROLOGICAL NOTICES FOR THE YEAR 1883.

By CHARLES HENRY HART, Historiographer.

CHARLES PERRIN SMITH.

Charles Perrin Smith, only son and third child of George Wishart and Hannah Carpenter [Ellet] Smith, was born in the City of Philadelphia, January 5th, 1819. His father was a Virginian, descended from the founders of that state, while his mother was a direct lineal descendant of Governor Thomas Lloyd and Samuel Carpenter, two of Penn's most able coadjutors in the settlement of Pennsylvania. Mr. and Mrs. Smith were married in Salem, N. J., where Mrs. Smith, then Miss Ellet, resided. Soon after the marriage they removed to Philadelphia, where the subject of this notice was born. Mr. Smith died while Charles Perrin was quite young, and Mrs. Smith returned with her family to her old home at Salem, and her son's future career is identified wholly with New Jersey.

In 1840, on attaining his majority, Charles Perrin Smith purchased a local newspaper called *The Banner*, and changing its name to *The National Standard*, became its editor and proprietor. He conducted it for eleven years, until 1851, when he retired from its management. In 1852 he was elected to represent Salem in the Senate of New Jersey, as an anti-railroad candidate, opposed to the usurpations and encroachments of that hydra-headed monster, the United Companies of New Jersey, now swallowed up by that yet more ravenous and dangerous one, the Pennsylvania Railroad Company. He served but one term, and in 1857 Governor Newell appointed him Clerk of the Supreme Court of New Jersey, when he removed his residence to Trenton, where he continued to reside until his death. He was twice re-appointed Clerk of the Court for terms of five years each, finally retiring in 1872.

In 1870, Mr. Smith printed for private distribution, his only permanent work; all of his many other writings being ephemeral contributions, in prose and verse, to the public press. This work was a quarto volume of eighty-eight pages, entitled *Lineage of the Lloyd and Carpenter Family.*

Compiled from authentic sources by Charles Perrin Smith, Trenton, N. J. For circulation among the Branches of the Family interested. Printed by S. Chew, Camden, 1870. Mr. Smith kindly presented me with a copy and also placed one in our library. In thanking him for his gift, I commented upon the fact that dates were so sparsely given throughout the book. In answer to which he writes, October 26, 1870: "I am much obliged for your kindly suggestions, and can only say that the omission of dates of births and deaths in reference to persons still living was intentional, as I am well aware of the sensitiveness manifested by many to such publicity. In other words, I desired peace and good will of all concerned." In 1871, Mr. Smith cancelled pages 51 and 52 of his original publication, substituting therefor, new and corrected matter; and in 1873, issued a nineteen page addenda to the *Lloyd Genealogy*, and a six page addenda to the *Carpenter Genealogy*.

During the summer of 1873, Mr. Smith, accompanied by his eldest daughter, made a journey abroad, and while in England, availed himself of an invitation to visit Wales, the ancient seat of the Lloyd family. Upon his return home, he wrote out his *Memoranda of a visit to the site of Mathraval Castle, Powys Castle, Valle Crucis Abbey, Pilar of Elisig, etc.*, which he issued in 1875, as a second addenda to the *Lloyd Lineage*. It covered twenty-four quarto pages, and was accompanied with a genealogical chart showing the descent of Thomas Lloyd from the ancient kings and princes of England and Wales. Mr. Smith subsequently made a second visit to England, in the hope that his broken health might be restored, but to no avail, and he died at his home in Trenton on the twenty-seventh of January, 1883.

Mr. Smith early identified himself with the old Whig party and took an active part in the Harrison Presidential campaign. About this time he travelled extensively through the West and Northwest, going over some six thousand miles, a graphic account of which he gave in a series of letters to the newspapers. He was active in the furtherance of all measures for the good of his adopted State, and during the war for the Union, rendered effective aid, as secret agent of the State, by appointment of Governor Olden. He was fond of aquatic sports, and during the summer usually cruised around in his own yacht. He had, too, considerable artistic taste, and his house was adorned with works of art, and graced with a fine library. He was a member of the Protestant Episcopal Church, and for several years a delegate to the Diocesan Convention.

In 1843, Mr. Smith was married at Salem to Hester A , daughter of Matthew Driver, of Caroline county, Maryland. Mrs. Smith, with two daughters, survive. Mr. Smith was elected a corresponding member of this Society, April 6th. 1871.

Lucius Quintius Cincinnatus Elmer.

Judge Elmer was born at Bridgeton, Cumberland County, New Jersey, February 3d, 1793. He was the oldest child and only son of General Ebenezer Elmer, a revolutionary patriot, by his wife Hannah Seeley, daughter of Colonel Ephraim and Hannah [Fithian] Seeley. General Elmer died October 18th, 1843, in his ninety second year, and was the last survivor of the original members of the Society of the Cincinnati of New Jersey, of which he was, for several years prior to his death, the President. It was owing to his interest in and connection with this society, that he named his son after the Roman Dictator from whom the Society took its name. The family name was originally Almyer, of whom one was Chief Baron of the Exchequer in 1535. John Alymer was tutor to the unfortunate Lady Jane Grey, and in 1568, was made Bishop of London by the name of John Elmer. The emigrant ancestor in this country was Edward Elmer, who came from England in 1632, with the company of forty-seven persons, comprising the church of Rev. Thomas Hooker and became one of the original proprietors of Hartford, Connecticut. He was killed by a straggling band of Indians during King Philip's war, in 1676. His second son Samuel (b. 1649. d. April 1691) had four children, the youngest of whom Daniel (b. 1689. d. Jan. 14, 1755) was one of the graduates from Yale College, at Saybrook, in 1713. The next year he removed to West Springfield, Mass, married and became a Presbyterian minister. About 1729 he came to Fairfield, Cumberland County, New Jersey, where he died. His eldest son, also Daniel (b. 1715 d. May 2, 1761) was the father of General Ebenezer Elmer, and grandfather of the subject of this notice.

L. Q. C. Elmer received his early education at the schools of Bridgeton. During the winter of 1803, he was sent to Woodbury to school, and the next year spent nine months at the boarding school of

Rev. Dr. Allison, at Bordentown. In 1804, when eleven years old, he witnessed the first exhibition of a magic-lantern he had ever seen. He had accompanied his father to Trenton to make a visit to Governor Bloomfield and his wife, who were childless, and for the entertainment of the youthful visitor, the magic-lantern was exhibited In the winter of 1811–12 he attended a partial course in this city at the University of Pennsylvania, and while there Dr. Jones was experimenting with Nitrous-oxide or laughing gas, which Dr. Redman Coxe had failed in. William M. Meredith was one of the party, and he stepped up to be experimented upon with the gas, but either did not take it properly or something occurred which caused a failure, and Elmer was selected as the second subject and upon him it was entirely successful, so that he was the first person in the city to take nitrous-oxide gas—now so universally used as an anæsthetic agent—with success. The year previous to this Mr. Elmer had been entered as a student at-law in the office of his cousin, Daniel Elmer, afterward a justice of the Supreme Court of New Jersey, for the term of five years required by the rules of court. On returning from his studies at Philadelphia, the war then recently declared against England was the exciting topic, and Mr. Elmer enrolled himself in the militia, became lieutenant of artillery, then Judge Advocate and later, Brigade Major and Inspector In May, 1815, he came up for examination for his license as an Attorney, before the Supreme Court, when Andrew Kirkpatrick was Chief Justice, and according to the usage at that period, called in person upon the Governor, who was also Chancellor, with his recommendation signed by the justices, and the Governor signed his commission. In May, 1818, he was licensed as a Counsellor and in 1834, called to be a Sergeant.

In the fall of 1820, Mr. Elmer was elected a member of the Assembly from the County of Cumberland, on a union ticket formed, in opposition to the regular democratic ticket, as an expression of adherence to the policy of President Monroe He was re-elected in 1821, 1822 and 1823, the last year being chosen Speaker. In 1824, President Monroe appointed him United States Attorney for New Jersey, which position he held until 1829, when he was superseded by President Jackson. The duties of the office were not very onerous, for in the five years he was District Attorney he had occasion to draw only one indictment, which was for obstructing the mail—the obstruction being that the defendant's horse could not trot so fast as Reeside's splendid team of full bloods, between Elizabeth and Newark. In 1843, Mr. Elmer was nominated by the democratic party as their candidate to represent the first district in Congress. At the preceding election the Whigs had succeeded in the district by about 1200 majority, and at the contest between Clay and Polk in 1844, carried it by 1500 majority. Mr. Elmer was elected by a majority of nearly 300, but was defeated at the following election. In 1850, he was made Attorney-General of the State, and held the position until 1852, when he was appointed a justice of the Supreme Court of New Jersey, and served the Constitutional term of seven years. After the death of Judge Clawson, in 1861, he was recalled to the same position by Gov. Olden, and continued in the active discharge of the duties of the office until 1869, when, his commission expiring, he declined a reappointment on account of advancing years, and withdrew entirely from public life and business. In addition to the positions already mentioned as filled by Judge Elmer, he was for many years Prosecutor of the Pleas for the counties of Cumberland and Cape May. He was also one of the joint commissioners with Richard Stockton, Theodore Frelinghuysen, James Parker and John Rutherford, appointed in 1827, by the Governor of New Jersey, for the settlement of the dispute with New York, respecting the waters dividing the two states. These commissioners had several conferences with the New York Commissioners, but failed to agree upon any terms of settlement. In 1833, new commissioners were appointed on the part of New York, and Frelinghuysen, Parker and Elmer were re-appointed for New Jersey. Judge Elmer was the one to propose the middle of the river as the true boundary line, and upon this basis the adjustment was made and ratified by the legislatures of both the States, and approved by the Congress of the United States.

Judge Elmer also made several important contributions to historical literature. In 1851, he delivered by request, before the Bench and Bar of New Jersey, an *Address upon the Life and Character of Hon. Garret D. Wall.* In 1860, he printed, in limited edition for the use of the family, *Geneaology* [*sic*] *and Biography of the Elmer Family,* which has been much sought after and has become so excessively scarce, that it was unknown to Mr. Whitmore when he published his American Genealogist in 1868.

In sending me a copy in 1871, he wrote: "I have been applied to for copies, even from London, which I could not send." In 1869, he published his *History of the Early Settlement and Progress of Cumberland County, New Jersey: and of the Currency of this and the adjoining Colonies.* Before the New Jersey Historical Society in May, 1870, he read a *History of the Constitution of New Jersey, adopted in* 1776, *and of the Government under it,* and by request of the same organization, he prepared a volume of five hundred pages entitled *The Constitution and Government of the Province and State of New Jersey, with Biographical Sketches of the Governors from* 1776 *to* 1845, *and Reminiscences of the Bench and Bar during more than half a century,* which was published in 1872, as Volume VII. of the Collections of the Society. He also published a *Digest of the Laws of New Jersey,* a *Book of Law Forms,* and contributed a short account of the *Titles to Land as held in New Jersey* to a new edition of his Digest, prepared by his son-in-law, the present United States District Judge, Hon. John T. Nixon. To a volume of local history entitled *The Pastor of the Old Stone Church,* he added a *Eulogy on Father Osborne,* as he was called, who when he died, May 1, 1858, lacked but three months and twenty days of being one hundred years old. At the Bi-Centennial celebration of the Old Stone Church, at Fairfield, September 29, 1880, he presided and made the opening address. He was then in his eighty-eighth year.

Judge Elmer did not have, as has been seen, a Collegiate education, but the College of New Jersey conferred upon him the honorary degree of Master of Arts in 1825, and in 1865 gave him the Doctorate of Laws. He was chosen a Trustee of the College in 1829, and continued to serve until 1864, when he resigned. He was admitted to succeed his father in the Society of the Cincinnati, July 4th, 1845, and at the time of his death was its President. He was elected a corresponding member of this Society, April 6th, 1871, and showed his interest in us by sending to our library, copies of his recent historical publications.

Judge Elmer was married in this city on October 6th, 1818, by the Rev. Mr. McCartee, Pastor of the Spruce Street Scotch Presbyterian Church, to Miss Catharine Hay. Her parents were from Dundee, who came over, after being married there, directly upon the close of the Revolutionary War, and settled in Philadelphia, where her father died of the yellow fever in 1793. Judge and Mrs. Elmer celebrated their Golden Wedding, or fiftieth anniversary of their marriage, in 1868, having present with them, on the occasion, all their children, (four daughters, two married and two single), and grand-children. He survived nearly fifteen years, and died of old age at his residence in Bridgeton, Sunday, March 11th, 1883, in his ninety-first year. The combined lives of father and son thus covered the great period of one hundred and eighty-two years. Judge Elmer in politics was a Democrat, but never was a strong partisan, and in religion, was as his family had been, a Presbyterian. He was a man of large information, genial in social intercourse, and was possessed of a strikingly handsome presence. I had the favor of his friendship for a number of years, and kept up an interesting correspondence with him for some time. The last time I had the pleasure of seeing him, was one day during the Centennial Exposition, when he came into my office to rest and chat. It was on this last occasion that I gleaned some of the data incorp rated in this sketch. Many of the letters that I have received from him would be most interesting to print, but want of space forbids it here.

George Sharswood.

George Sharswood was born in Philadelphia, July 7, 1810. His ancestor, George Sharswood, an English emigrant, settled in New London, Connecticut, about 1665. The family subsequently removed to Cape May, New Jersey, and here George Sharswood, the great-grandfather of the subject of this notice and the grandson of the emigrant, was born October 18th, 1696. When a boy of ten he was brought to Philadelphia, and August 17, 1722, was married, at the First Presbyterian Church, to Mary Whatley. He married a second time April 30, 1747, at Christ Church, Philadelphia, Anne Topp, and his eldest child by his second marriage, James Sharswood, was born in Philadelphia, March 27, 1748. He received his education at the Philadelphia Academy, under the Rev. Mr Beveridge, and then, as it was the custom in those days to bring young men up to a trade, was apprenticed to a house carpenter. He did not however follow his trade, but engaged largely in the lumber business and amassed a considerable fortune. He married April 2d, 1775, Elizabeth daughter of Joseph Bredin of Abington, Bucks County, Pennsylvania. He was a man of consideration and commanded a company of Associators in the brilliant movement against Trenton in December 1776.

He was one of the original members of the Democratic, then called Republican, party, the first regular organization of which was in Philadelphia in 1796, in an unsuccessful attempt to oust the Federalists from the City Government. He was a member of Select Council and afterwards of the State Legislature; and Governor Snyder offered him, in 1809, the Commission of associate or lay Judge of the Common Pleas Court. He was the author of various articles adverse to the Bank of the United States, which were published in *The Aurora* newspaper, in 1817, under the signature of *Nestor,* and afterward collected into a pamphlet. He died September 14th, 1836, in his eighty-ninth year. He had several children, but only two reached maturity, one of whom was George, the father of the subject of this notice, who died February 2d, 1810, at the early age of 22, five months and five days before the birth of his son.

George Sharswood, familiarly known for more than a third of a century as Judge Sharswood, was brought up and educated under the immediate care of his grandfather; and was graduated from the University of Pennsylvania, on the 31st of July, 1828, with the highest honors, delivering the Greek salutatory. In less than a month after leaving college, he was entered as a student of law in the office of the Hon. Joseph R. Ingersoll, and was admitted to practice September 5, 1831, two months after he attained his majority. In 1834, he published the first of a long series of contributions from his pen to the literature and learning of his profession, being an article in the *American Quarterly Review* for June, on *The Revised Code of Pennsylvania.* The year following he was elected President of the Law Academy of Philadelphia. The same year he gave to the profession the first fruit of his editorial labors, in an annotated edition of *Roscoe's Digest of the Law of Evidence in Criminal Cases,* which has since gone through seven editions. In 1837, he was elected a member of the legislature of the State, and this service was followed by a term of three years in the Select Council of Philadelphia. In 1841 and 1842, he was again sent to the legislature, and the *Journal of the House of Representatives* shows him to have been one of the active working members of that body. The affairs of the United States Bank having about this time become much involved, a committee of stockholders was chosen to examine its condition, of which George Sharswood was made Secretary. He prepared the report and was also the author of the second report of this committee, designed to answer attacks upon the former report.

The main labors of his life however, were connected with the bench, which he adorned by his ability, scholarship and impartial spirit. His publications, his public service and his growing reputation as a lawyer, made him warmly welcomed by the bar and the people, when Governor Shunk nominated him on April 8, 1845, as associate Justice of the District Court for the City and County of Philadelphia. The nomination was immediately and unanimously confirmed by the Senate, and the next day he took his seat upon the bench, being not quite thirty-five years of age. Upon the resignation of Judge Joel Jones in February, 1848, to accept the presidency of Girard College, Judge Sharswood was created President Judge of the Court. In 1851, the judiciary having been made elective, he was returned to the bench by the unanimous vote of all parties, having been nominated by five conventions successively, the Democrats, Whigs, Native Americans, and the Temperance and Workingmen's parties. He was re-elected for a second term of ten years in 1861, but before he had served out his term, he was elevated to the Supreme Court. On April 2d, 1850, Judge Sharswood was selected by the Trustees of the University of Pennsylvania, Professor of Law, and his first lecture was delivered in the old University building on Ninth Street, September 30th, 1850, on the *Profession of the Law*. The chair had not been filled for a quarter of a century, and the duties entailed the building up of the school. Mr. Carson in his *Historical Sketch of the Law Department of the University*, prefaced to the Catalogue of the Alumni says: "The interest awakened by the revival of the department was greater than could have been anticipated. The reputation of the lecturer at once re-established the school, and he found himself attended by members of the bar in active practice, as well as by undergraduates." The duties soon became too onerous for one man to discharge and it was determined to increase the faculty to three, and on May 4th, 1852, Judge Sharswood was elected Professor of the Institutes of Law, and Dean of the Faculty; Mr. Peter McCall, Professor of Pleading Practice and Evidence, and Mr. E. Spencer Miller, Professor of the Law of Real Estate and Equity Jurisprudence. Judge Sharswood continued his lectures twice a week, the course extending over two years, until, when upon taking his seat on the bench of the Supreme Court, he resigned, January 23, 1868. He, however, continued his course of lectures until it became necessary for him to leave the city to sit with the Supreme Court at Harrisburg, and his final lecture was delivered on the last day of April, 1868. The occasion was both impressive and interesting. At the conclusion of the lecture the classes of 1867 and '68 presented to the lecturer a massive silver fruit dish, as a token of their esteem, together with a series of resolutions expressive of their appreciation, not only of the instruction they had received, but of the uniform courtesy and kindness he had ever extended to them. These were received in a most feeling manner, coupled with the request that he might be permitted to clasp the hand of each one present before parting. So closed his professional connection with the University of Pennsylvania.

Judge Sharswood was a great common-law lawyer and a great judge at *Nisi Prius*, and many have doubted, notwithstanding his immense learning and eminent judicial qualifications, whether his usefulness was not impaired by his elevation to the bench of the Supreme Court. It was, however, a fitting complement to his judicial life, and a fitting recognition of his attainments as a jurist, when the people of the State at large chose him, in the fall of 1867, to succeed Chief Justice Woodward. He was nominated by the Democratic party; and in a year of Republican majorities all over the country and in his own state, he was elected over his Republican opponent, who held a like position to his own in Allegheny County. He took his seat upon the Supreme bench the first Monday in January, 1868, and on January 6th, 1879, by priority of commission became Chief Justice of the Supreme Court of Pennsylvania, a worthy successor of Tilghman and Gibson. His commission, for the period he was elected, fifteen years, expired with the last day of last year, and Chief Justice Sharswood retired from public life. Upon this occasion the bar of Philadelphia tendered him a complimentary reception and dinner, which was given at the Academy of Music on December 20th, 1882, and was one of the most notable social gatherings ever held in this city. The proceedings on this occasion have been preserved in a beautiful pamphlet, prefixed to which is a striking likeness of the Judge.

Judge Sharswood was now in his seventy-third year and for many,

many years had been an intense sufferer from a terrible malady—indeed, during his last fifteen years of official life, he said himself, he never had a waking hour that he was free from suffering. This was physical pain; added to it he had deep mental suffering. He had married November 27th, 1849, Mary, daughter of the Hon. George Chambers of Chambersburg, Pa., sometime a Justice of the Supreme Court of Pennsylvania. She died November 8th, 1857, leaving him an only child, a son, for whom he had the brightest hopes. He told our venerated President (Eli K. Price), who was also his examiner for admission to the bar, soon after his election to the Supreme Court, that he should not live through his term; that his sufferings were so great that he had no desire to live longer than the five years that would bring his son to lawful age and to the bar. His hopes here too, were not to be fulfilled. The son fell a victim to the ravages of consumption and preceded his father to the grave. His venerable mother, whose maiden name was Esther Dunn, and who had always been one of his household, died January 13th, 1865, at the ripe age of eighty-three. Therefore, considering his years and his trials, and his sufferings it was no surprise to his friends—and they were all who knew him or had come in contact with him—to hear, that with the untying of his buckler and the laying aside of his official robes, his health was rapidly failing; and when on the 28th of May, 1883, it was announced that Judge Sharswood was dead, the members of the Philadelphia bar, old and young, each individually felt he had met with a personal loss that could not readily be repaired; the universal feeling was, that *he was a man, take him for all in all, we shall not look upon his like again.*

Judge Sharswood's kindness to the young men who were entering the profession was proverbial, and he made them feel that he was their friend and would be their counsellor. I first knew him when in the fall of 1866, I was enrolled a student-at-law and attended his lectures at the University, and from that time until his death my intercourse with him, both professional and social, was of the most agreeable character. When I entered upon my professional career, from him I received my first substantial encouragement. From *Nisi Prius*, soon after my admission, he referred to me an equity cause as Examiner, and subsequently enlarged my powers to that of Master. When I began dallying with letters he was among the first to give me warm encouragement. To show the genial, kindly, yet critical spirit he conveyed it in, I transcribe extracts from two of his letters. In the first, written in the spring of 1868, he says: "I thank you for your Memoir of Prescott. It is written with great justice and discrimination in the thoughts, and with an elegant simplicity of style which is truly Addisonian. I trust you will continue in the course on which you have entered with so much promise." The second came to me in the fall of 1871. He writes: "I thank you for a copy of your Memoir of George Ticknor, which you have had the politeness to send to me, and for the kind manner in which it has been done. I have read it with great interest and pleasure as a very earnest and eloquent tribute to the Memory of one of whom, as Americans, we must all feel proud. I trust you will continue in the course you have so honorably begun—turning aside occasionally from the rugged road of the profession to the pleasant side walks of literature." Such words as these coming from such a fountain source are not to be forgotten.

Judge Sharswood always took a deep interest in the Law Academy of Philadelphia. He early became a member, and as has already been stated, was elected President for the season 1836-37. In 1838, he was elected one of the Vice-Provosts, which position he held until 1855, when he was chosen Provost to succeed Judge Sergeant, an office he continued to hold through life. On the 19th of September, 1855, he delivered before the Academy, a lecture on *The Common Law of Pennsylvania*, and his last appearance in public, was when on March 13th, 1883, he addressed the members again, by special request, on *The Origin, History and Objects of the Law Academy of Philadelphia.* It was while he was preparing this address, that I saw him for the last time, except afterward casually on the street. He came to me to know if I could help him with some data respecting Judge Thomas Sergeant, a brief sketch of whom he wanted to incorporate in his address. Unfortunately, I had nothing that was new to him.

Judge Sharswood was emphatically a student, and his views upon the best methods of study, both for the teacher and the learner, are embodied in three carefully considered and well thought out addresses before his *Alma Mater;* December 10th, 1856, and again January 18th, 1869, before the Society of the Alumni, and December 17th, 1872, before the Philomathean Society of the University of Pennsylvania. These have been printed, and will well repay a perusal. His other literary essays not immediately connected with his profession, are three necrologies read before the American Philosophical Society, one in October, 1860, upon Judge Joel Jones, another in October, 1863, upon Charles J. Ingersoll, and the third in December, 1868, upon his preceptor in the law, the Hon. Joseph R. Ingersoll.

Judge Sharswood's literary work was chiefly as an annotator. His original contributions to legal literature—excepting of course the enormous number of his judicial opinions during a career of nearly thirty-eight years upon the Bench—are merely gatherings from his lectures. In 1854, he published his essay on *Professional Ethics: a Compend of Lectures on the Aims and Duties of the Profession of the Law*, which was "To my honored master, Joseph R. Ingersoll, LL. D. Inscribed as a testimony of respect and gratitude." A second edition was issued in 1860, with an introduction prefixed on the *Importance of the Profession of the Law in a Public point of View*. In my copy of this edition, I have the pleasure of reading, in his peculiar hand-writing, "*Charles H. Hart, Esq., from Geo. Sharswood.*" I need not add how much I prize it. He gave it to me one day after lecture, saying that I might find in it some thoughts that would be useful to me, and needless to say, that I, in common with all who have read this masterly thesis on a not very easy theme, have found many thoughts of much use and ever increasing importance to be disseminated throughout the Bar. Two subsequent editions of *Professional Ethics* have appeared. In 1856, was published his *Popular Lectures on Commercial Law*, which had originally been prepared for the students of Crittenden's Commercial College. While professor in the University, he delivered many introductory lectures, a selection of which was published in 1870, under the title of *Lectures Introductory to the Study of the Law*.

As has been said, Judge Sharswood's literary work was chiefly as an annotator, but his annotations have made known and valuable some text books that would have been unknown on this side of Ocean without them. Not so however with his chiefest work, which is too, his chiefest glory. In 1859, after many years of assiduous labor, he published his edition of *Blackstone's Commentaries on the Laws of England, with Notes and a Life of the Author*. It was prepared with special reference to the use of American lawyers, and was immediately adopted as the edition of Blackstone to be used throughout the breadth and length of the land, by all students of the law. Nor did it stop here. It crossed the water and took its place along side of the editions of Archbold, Christian and Chitty in the libraries of British lawyers. The number of copies printed and sold of this work must count by the tens of thousands. He annotated also *Russell on Crimes and Misdemeanors*, 1836; *Leigh's Abridgment of the Law of Nisi Prius*, 1838; *Stephens' Law of Nisi Prius Evidence*, 1844; *Byles' Law of Bills of Exchange and Promissory Notes*, 1853, his preface and notes to which were republished by the author in the eighth English edition of his work, and acknowledged in high terms of commendation. *Smith's Law of Contracts*, 1856; *Starkie's Law of Evidence*, 1860; and *Tudor's Leading Cases in Mercantile and Maritime Law, with American Notes and References*, 1873. All of these works have gone through several editions. In addition to the above, in conjunction with his early and life-long friend, Mr. George W. Biddle, he prepared an index to the first forty-seven volumes of the *English Common Law Reports*, 1847. In 1853, he began editing the *English Common Law Reports*, and annotated the volumes from 66 to 90. He also edited volumes 4, 5 and 6 of the *British Crown Cases*, and a continuation of *Story's Public and General Statutes passed by the Congress of the United States*, from 1828 to 1846, volumes 4 and 5. At the time of his decease, he was engaged with Mr. Henry Budd, upon *Leading Cases in the American Law of Real Property*, the first volume of which he lived to see published.

He was for many years President of the Philadelphia Institution for the Deaf and Dumb, and in 1872, was elected a Trustee of his *Alma Mater*. From 1872, to the time of his death he was also President of the Society of the Alumni of the University of Pennsylvania. In 1856, the University of the City of New York and Columbia College, honored themselves by conferring upon him the Doctorate of Law. In 1875, the Alumni of the Law Department of the University, founded a money prize for the best essay, by the graduating class, each year and appropriately named it in his honor, "the Sharswood Prize." Shortly after he had left the Chief Justiceship, and the present administration of the State came into power, it was thought well to appoint a Commission to codify the Acts of Assembly, and Judge Sharswood was placed at its head. Judge Sharswood was an earnest member of the Presbyterian Church. He was a Trustee of the Tabernacle Presbyterian Church, in this city, from 1832 until 1872, serving a portion of the time as Secretary, and then President of the Board. He was a Trustee of the General Assembly of the Church, and Director of the Theological Seminary at Princeton. He was elected an Honorary Member of this Society, April 2nd, 1868, being only the second resident of this city so enrolled; the other being the eminent bibliographer, Dr. S. Austin Allibone, now residing in New York.

This is but an outline of his career. To fill up the skeleton would require a volume, rather than these scant pages.

DONATIONS HAVE BEEN RECEIVED DURING THE YEAR FROM THE FOLLOWING:

I.—Individuals.

* Ambrosoli, Solone	Como, Italy.
Allen, John K.	Lansing, Michigan.
* Arnold, Isaac N.	Chicago, Illinois.
* Adams, Herbert B.	Baltimore, Maryland.
Ambiveri, Luigi	Piacenza, Italy.
* Brooks, Rev. W. H.	Hanover, New Hampshire.
* Black, Wm. George	Glasgow, Scotland.
* Brown, Miss Marie A.	Stockholm, Sweden.
Burns, C. de F.	New York City, N. Y.
Beers, W. A.	Fairfield, Connecticut.
Bahrfeldt, M.	Berlin, Prussia.
* Burchard, Horatio C., Director U. S. Mint.	Washington, D. C.
* Butler, James D.	Madison, Wisconsin.
* Bergsoë, Sophus A.	Copenhagen, Denmark.
* Bojnivic, Ivan von	Agram, Austria.
* Barber, Edwin Atlee	Philadelphia.
* Bradlee, Rev. Caleb Davis	Boston, Massachusetts.
* Baker, John R.	Philadelphia.
* Brinton, Dr. Daniel G.	Philadelphia.
* Culin, R. Stewart	Philadelphia.
* Da Silva, Chev. J. P.	Lisbon, Portugal.
* Devilliers, Leopold	Mons, Belgium.
* De Cleve, Jules	Mons, Belgium.
* Davis, Robert Coulton	Philadelphia.
* Evans, John	Hemel Hempstead, England.
* ———, Walton W.	New Rochelle, N. Y.
Eaton, John	Washington, D. C.
Gebert, C. F.	Nurnberg, Baiern.
* Galati, the Prince of	Palermo, Italy.
* Gatschet, Dr. Albert S.	Washington, D. C.
Goddard, Dr. and Mrs. Kingston	Philadelphia.
* Homes, Henry A.	Albany, N. Y.
* Horner, Dr. Frederick	Salem, Virginia.
Hess, Adolph, ...	Fkft. a m.

* Horstman, G. Harry . . . . Nurnberg, Bavaria.
* Hale, Horatio . . . . Clinton, Canada.
Hahlo, Julius . . . . Fkft. a m.
* Harden, Wm. . . . . Savannah, Georgia.
* Hart, Charles Henry . . . . . . Philadelphia.
* Haseltine, Jno. W. . . . . Philadelphia.
* Haynes, Henry W. . . . . Boston, Mass.
* Hayden, Rev. Horace Edwin . . . . . . Wilkes-Barrè, Pennsylvania.
* Hockley, Thomas . . . . Philadelphia.
* Hildebrand, Bror Emil . . . . Stockholm, Sweden.
* Imhoof-Blumer, Dr. F. . . . . Winterthur, Switzerland.
* Jones, Charles C., Jr. . . . . Augusta, Georgia.
* ———, Dr. Joseph . . . . New Orleans, Louisiana.
* Jenkins, Howard M. . . . . West Chester, Pennsylvania.
* Koehler, S. R. . . . . Roxbury, Massachusetts.
———, K. F. . . . . Leipzig.
* Lundy, Rev. John P. . . . . Philadelphia.
Lawrence, Rd. Hoe . . . . New York City, N. Y.
* Lewis, H. Carvill . . . . Philadelphia.
* Le Moine, J. M. . . . . Quebec, Canada.
Littlefield, G. E. . . . . Boston, Massachusetts.
Medal, Dr. Melasio . . . . Patzacuaro, Mexico.
* Muoni, Cav. Damiano . . . . Milan, Italy.
* Macedo, Dr. . . . . Lima, Peru.
* Merzbacher, Dr. E. . . . . Munich, Bavaria.
* Olaguibel, Manuel de . . . . Mexico, Mexico.
* Pomialowski, I. . . . . St. Petersburg, Russia.
* Powell, Major J. W. . . . . Washington, D. C.
* Price, Eli K. . . . . Philadelphia.
* Preble, Admiral George Henry . . . . . Brookline, Mass.
Phillips, Miss Emily . . . . Philadelphia.
* Putnam, Frederick W. . . . . Cambridge, Massachusetts.
* Postolacca, Chev. A. . . . . Athens, Greece.
* Phillips, Henry, Jr. . . . . Philadelphia.
Perry, Amos . . . . Providence, Rhode Island.
Quaritch, Bernard . . . . London, England.
* Rau, Dr. Charles . . . . Washington, D. C.
* Richards, A. E. . . . . Florence, Italy.
* Rosny, Leon de . . . . Paris, France.
* Seletti, Emiliò . . . . Milan.
Smith, A. Lewis . . . . Philadelphia.
Smith, H. W. . . . . Philadelphia.

Schulerman, J. . . . . Amersfort, Holland.
*Thomas, T. H. . . . . Cardiff, Wales.
Thiemé, C. G. . . . . Leipzig.
*Taylor, Alfred B. . . . . Philadelphia.
*Tiesenhausen, W. von . . . . St. Petersburgh.
Townsend, Washington . . . . West Chester, Pa.
*Trübner, Nicholas . . . . London.
Wickersham, Dr. Morris J. . . . . Piacenza, Italy.
*Winthrop, Robert C. . . . . Boston, Mass.
*Whittlesey, Charles E. . . . . Cleveland, Ohio.
*Whitehead, William A. . . . . Newark, N. J.
Wesener, F. J. . . . . Munich, Bavaria.

II.—Societies, Etc.

American Philosophical Society . . . . . . Philadelphia.
Accademia deí Lincei . . . . Rome, Italy.
Accademia fisio-medico-statistica di Milano, Italy.
Accademia di Palermo . . . . Sicily, Italy.
Academie de Lisbon . . . . Lisbon, Portugal.
Academy of Sciences . . . . Davenport, Iowa.
Academy of Sciences . . . . St. Louis, Mo.
Academy of Sciences . . . . Madison, Wisconsin.
Bodleian Library . . . . Oxford, England.
Bureau of Education . . . . Washington, D. C.
Berlin Numismatische Gesellschaft . . . . Berlin, Prussia.
Baierische Numismatische Gesellschaft . . . Munich, Bavaria.
Brooklyn Library . . . . Brooklyn, N. Y.
Cambridge Antiquarian Society . . . . . Cambridge, England.
Cercle Archeologique . . . . Mons, Belgique.
Essex Institute . . . . Salem, Massachusetts.
Glasgow Archæological Society . . . . . Glasgow, Scotland.
Glasgow Philosophical Society . . . . . Glasgow, Scotland.
Historical Societies of Delaware, Georgia, Maryland, New Jersey, New Mexico, Western Reserve, Wisconsin, Wyoming Hist. and Geol.
Institution Ethnographique de France . . Paris, France.
London Numismatic Society . . . . . . London, England.
Munich Antiquarian Society (Alt. Verein) Munich, Bavaria.
Musèe Guimèt . . . . Lyon, France.
Musèe du Louvre . . . . Paris, France.
Montreal Numismatic & Archælogical Soc'y. Montreal, Canada.

New York State Library . . . . Albany, New York.
New York Numismatic & Archæologic'l Soc. New York.
Pennsylvania Museum, &c. . . . . Philadelphia.
Peabody Museum . . . . Cambridge, Massachusetts.
Philadelphia Library Co. . . . . Philadelphia.
Smithsonian Institution . . . . Washington, D. C.
Sociètè Imperiale d'Archeologie Russe . . . St. Petersburg, Russia.
Vienna Numismatische Gesellschaft . . . Vienna, Austria.

www.ingramcontent.com/pod-product-compliance
Lightning Source LLC
Chambersburg PA
CBHW021548270326
41930CB00008B/1414

* 9 7 8 3 7 4 1 1 9 8 0 0 7 *